JAN 1 1 2017

W9-CPB-911

Pet Food Tester

ODD JOBS

VIRGINIA LOH-HAGAN

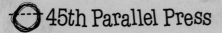
45th Parallel Press

Published in the United States of America by Cherry Lake Publishing
Ann Arbor, Michigan
www.cherrylakepublishing.com

Content Adviser: Philip Wells, Technical consultant, Cambridge UK
Reading Adviser: Marla Conn MS, Ed., Literacy specialist, Read-Ability, Inc.

Photo Credits: © cynoclub/Shutterstock, cover, 1; © Solo/ZUMA Press/Newscom, 5; © pathdoc/Shutterstock, 6; © Africa Studio/Shutterstock, 9; © Leah-Anne Thompson/Shutterstock, 11; © IS_ImageSource/istock, 13; © Fuse/Thinkstock, 14; © monkeybusinessimages/Thinkstock, 17; © bo1982/Thinkstock, 19; 21 Corbis tk; © Serdar Tibet/Shutterstock, 23; © saiko3p/Shutterstock, 25; © Ryan McVay/Thinkstock, 27, 28; © ARENA Creative/Shutterstock, cover, multiple interior pages; © oculo/Shutterstock, multiple interior pages; © Denniro/Shutterstock.com, cover, multiple interior pages; © PhotoHouse/Shutterstock, multiple interior pages; © Miloje/Shutterstock, multiple interior pages

Copyright © 2017 by Cherry Lake Publishing
All rights reserved. No part of this book may be reproduced or utilized in any form or by any means without written permission from the publisher.

45th Parallel Press is an imprint of Cherry Lake Publishing.

Library of Congress Cataloging-in-Publication Data

CIP data has been filed and is available at catalog.loc.gov

Cherry Lake Publishing would like to acknowledge the work of The Partnership for 21st Century Skills. Please visit *www.p21*.org for more information.

Printed in the United States of America
Corporate Graphics Inc.

Contents

CHAPTER 1

Pet Heroes

**Who are some famous pet food testers?
How do they help pets?**

Simon Allison has three cats. He wants them to have good food. He's a pet food tester. His **palate** is special. Palate is a sense of taste. He knows what pets like.

He looks for things that shouldn't be in the food. Pet food can't have hair, horns, hooves, or poop. Pet food must come from muscles. It can also come from tongues, throats, or hearts.

He sniffs the food. He chews for a bit. He doesn't swallow. He doesn't want to get fat. He doesn't want bad breath. He rinses his mouth. He chews gum.

His favorite is a cat food dish. It has chicken and vegetables.

Pet food testers are also known as food technologists or pet food critics.

3 0053
01196
5426

Edwin Rose likes eating pet food. He said, "The **ingredients** are so good." Ingredients are the things in a food dish.

He works for a grocery store. He tests their pet foods. He's tasted 300 items. He learned pets don't like cold food. Cold ruins the smell. He learned pets like **organ** meats.

Aroma is how something smells.

Spotlight Biography
LUCY POSTINS

Lucy Postins loves dogs. She has two Rhodesian Ridgebacks and a pug. She wants her pets to have high-quality food. She started her own company. It's called The Honest Kitchen. She makes food that improves pets' skin, fur, and health. Her dog food includes free-range chicken, ranch-raised beef, sweet potatoes, eggs, bananas, and dandelion greens. She tastes every ingredient. She also tastes the finished products. She makes sure the food tastes "just right." She tests for flavor, smell, and color. She checks for freshness. She said, "Some of my friends think it's an odd thing to do but most of them have pets they love as much as—or in some cases maybe even more than—their own children. So [they] can see where I'm coming from."

Rose didn't start on pet food. He started with canned fish. Then, he tested sugar and olive oil.

Rose's wife said, "I've bought him countless mouthwashes and toothpastes. But it doesn't get rid of that meaty smell."

Mark Gooley is a pet food tester. He owns a company. He makes pet food. He makes food for dogs and horses.

He tastes doggy dental sticks. He tastes chewy bones. He likes soft food best.

He wants pets to enjoy eating. He said, "If you wouldn't put it in your mouth, don't you dare expect your dog to eat it."

He has an odd job. He said, "It's like being a mad scientist … I wouldn't do anything else." Pet food testers are heroes to pets. They ensure pet food is healthy. They ensure it tastes good.

Pet food testers look for texture. This is how something feels.

CHAPTER 2

Yummy in the Tummy

What do pet food testers do? What are the different types of pet food testers?

Pets can't talk. So, people eat pet food. They get paid to talk about it. Pet food testers study the food. They work in a lab. They study the taste. They study the content. They rate the flavor. They rate how it feels. They take notes. They write reports. They suggest changes. They improve the food. They share ideas. Only the best pet food is sent to stores.

Pet food testers chew slowly. They figure out the ingredients. Most spit out the food. They don't eat it. They taste several items at a time. They taste food over and over again. They test more than taste.

Pet food testing is a food science.

Pet food testers have good **taste buds**. Taste buds are small bumps. They're on tongues. Taste buds sense flavors. There are five basic flavors. They're sweet, sour, salty, bitter, and **umami**. Umami means savory. Taste is the sum of flavors.

Pet food testers do more than taste. They smell. Smell is important. It draws pets. It's why pets eat. Pets won't eat food that smells bad. Pet owners won't serve it.

Pet food testers want pets to be happy. They want owners to be happy. They ensure food looks good. They ensure food smells good.

There are different types of food testers. Assistants make general notes. They taste everything. They prepare the food. Testers make the official reports. They spend more time on each item. Directors listen to testers. They create new recipes.

Pet food also has to appeal to pet owners.

Jon Hanson is a cat food quality controller. He gets a big tub. It's filled with cat food. He puts his face in it. He ensures it's fresh. He puts his arms in the tub. He looks for bones. He removes bones. He scoops out some cat food. He smears it on a surface. He ensures there's no **gristle**. Gristle is the tough meat bits.

Ingredients are the things that go into a food product.

Pet Food Tester
KNOW THE LINGO

Cheap pellet: kibble that has grains

FDA: U.S. Food and Drug Administration

Flavoring: taste enhancer

Guaranteed analysis: the right amounts of nutrients listed on food labels

Kibble: dry pet food, crumbled dog biscuits

Lamb meal: dry protein from the meat of lambs

Meal: dry protein material that is made by cooking the fats out of meat and then drying it into a flour

Meat: muscle meat

Meat by-products: animal parts like lungs, spleens, kidneys, livers, blood, bones, fat, and stomachs

Meat meal: dry protein from the meat of cattle, pigs, sheep, or goats

Poultry by-products: animal parts like lungs, spleens, kidneys, livers, blood, bones, fat, and stomachs of chickens or turkeys

Poultry meal: dry protein from the meat of chickens or turkeys

Rendering: process by which animal parts are heated slowly over a long period of time so the fat can be removed

Wet food: canned meat with gravy or jelly; or loaf style with little jelly and no gravy

CHAPTER 3

Taking the First Bite

How do people become pet food testers?
What do they need?

Pet food testers are willing to eat pet food. Not many people will do this.

Philip Wells works for Lily's Kitchen. It's a pet food company. He said, "Taste is an important quality to check to ensure each different ingredient is perfectly balanced in just the right way."

Philip said there are some "pretty **gruesome** pet foods out there." Gruesome means gross. Philip ensures these foods don't get put in stores.

He likes his job. He helps pets. He gets to work with Lily. Lily is a dog.

Pet food companies hire testers.

Some pet food testers worked in food businesses. Some were cooks. They understand food. Some pet food testers studied at school. They studied nutrition. They studied food science. But they get trained on the job. They learn to identify flavors. They learn what pets like. They learn what pets don't like.

Pet food testers have certain traits. They pay attention to details. They study information. They solve

Advice From the Field
CAMI HAWKINSON

Cami Hawkinson works for The Honest Kitchen. She does research and development. She advises hiring pet food tasters. She said, "Tasting our pet food is vitally important to us. We simply wouldn't feed our own animals a product that we couldn't eat ourselves." Testers taste the completed pet food. They also taste each individual ingredient. The company's pet food can be eaten by humans. It's called human grade pet food. Officials inspect every ingredient. It's important to please the pets. The company also gets dogs to test the food.

problems. They give honest feedback. They write well. They speak well.

There are many pet food companies. Some hire pet food testers. These companies tend to have high-quality pet food.

Pet food testers always have animals' best interests in mind.

CHAPTER 4

From Scraps to Store Shelves

How did the pet food business develop and change? What happened in 2007? Who studied how to study pet food?

In the past, pets ate raw meat. They ate **scraps**. Scraps are leftovers. They're food that humans didn't finish eating. Then, things changed. People changed the way they fed pets.

James Pratt was a salesman. He was from Ohio. He went to London. He went in the late 1800s. He saw

British sailors throwing "hard tack." They were feeding it to stray dogs. Hard tack is a biscuit. It's made of flour, water, and salt. He got an idea. He made dog cakes. These became the first dog biscuits.

Companies canned pet food. In World War II, metal was not always available. Companies couldn't make cans. So, they invented dry pet food.

The invention of Spam helped create the canned pet food business.

WHEN ODD IS TOO ODD!

Eating cat food is odd. Eating cats is odder. Martin Bühlmann is from Switzerland. Switzerland allows people to eat cats and dogs. It's one of the few countries in Europe that allow this. He cooks and eats cats. He said cat meat is "delicate and easily digestible." To him, cats taste good. They're easy to eat. He said, "It tastes better than rabbits." Bühlmann is over 70 years old. He likes to eat the food his grandmother made. He eats pig's ear, calf's brain, foxes, and badgers. He grew up in a large, poor family. His mother cooked cat meat. It was meat they could get. But he won't eat dogs. It's because he had a dog. The dog's name was Julian.

World War II ended. People spent more money. More companies made pet food. They made different kinds. Stores offered many choices.

Now there are many laws about making pet food. Food must be cooked at a high temperature. It has to be cooked for a long time. Companies have to check the food. But something bad happened. It started in early 2007. Pets ate bad food. Over 3,600 pets died.

Almost 500 pets had kidney problems. They got really sick. More pets got sick. More pets died.

One company **recalled** the bad food. Recall means to have people return things. More companies recalled their food. Over 100 types of pet food were recalled.

Unhealthy pet food made pets sick. Pet owners wanted more rules for the making of pet food.

People were mad. They wanted more laws. They wanted pet food to be checked better.

Dr. Gary Pickering is a professor. He studied a way to test canned cat food. He did this in 2007. He put together a group of taste testers. First, he used regular food. Then, he brought out cat food. Some of his testers quit. Others liked the cat food. Testers tested for 18 flavors.

Dr. Timothy J. Bowser studies pet food. He thinks humans are good at testing some things. Humans can test for smell, look, and feel. But he prefers using pets as testers. He said, "Getting the opinion directly from the pet is much more accurate than working indirectly through humans."

Offal is a cat food flavor. It's a blend of boiled and finely cut beef kidney and liver.

CHAPTER 5

Lowdown on the Chowdown

What are some problems with pet food?
What are some solutions?

Some people have a problem with pet food. They question pet food companies. A long time ago some companies used bad meat. They used sick or dead animals. They used animals they shouldn't use. Some used zoo animals. Some used **roadkill**. Roadkill are animals killed by cars. Some used other cats and dogs. Luckily, this is no longer legal.

Some people don't like the process. Animals are killed. People think it's inhumane. Inhumane means not kind. People think the animals suffer.

Some pet owners make their own food. They use real ingredients. Some only buy **premium** pet food. This means top-quality items.

Humans want their pets to have healthy food.

Richard Thompson has his own company. He uses fresh ingredients. He created refrigerated dog meals. His pet food smells like human food. He said, "This is the next level of how people are going to feed their pets."

More companies are creating pet food that humans can eat. This makes pet food testing easier. It's still an odd job. But it doesn't have to be an icky job.

THAT HAPPENED?!?

Humans aren't the only ones who taste pet food. Bears do, too. A bear in New Jersey broke into a house. The bear was 200 pounds (90.7 kilograms). It broke through a window. It found a bag of cat food. It also ate Peppermint Patties. It spat the wrappers on the floor. It left through the same window. Another bear couldn't resist pet food. This bear was in Florida. It broke into a man's garage. It ate a 20 pound (9 kg) bag of dog food. It ate for 30 minutes. Then it went to the neighbor's backyard. The bear was full. It took a nap. It slept for an hour. Bob Cross saw the bear. He said, "It laid all the way down. And the thing just rolled right over." It woke up. It walked into the woods.

DID YOU KNOW?

- Canned dog food has more meat than dry dog food. But dry is just as healthy.

- Some pets, especially cats, don't drink enough water. Wet pet food gives them extra water.

- Supertasters have more taste buds. They have an excellent sense of taste. Women are more likely to be supertasters. People from Asia, South America, and Africa are also more likely to be supertasters.

- Humans can eat pet food. But pets can't eat all human food. Pets can't eat chocolate, coffee, soda, raisins, grapes, some nuts, garlic, or onions. Pets could die.

- Pets shouldn't eat too much. They don't hunt anymore. So, they don't get much exercise. They could get fat.

- Creating cat food came after dog food. Cats are able to hunt. Cats could take care of themselves more than dogs.

- In the 1800s and early 1900s, horse meat was sold as pet food. In London, people sold horse meat from handcarts. They were called Cats' Meat Men.

- Cats don't eat grains by choice. So, cat food makers add special flavors. They want to get cats to eat the food.

- Some pets eat poop. This is called coprophagy. This could mean they're sick. In some cases, it's normal. Mother cats and dogs eat their babies' poop. This is how they clean their babies.

- Marilyn vos Savant has the highest IQ ever recorded. If she were stuck, she'd eat dog food. She said, "It's formulated with the intention of covering all the dietary needs of one healthy animal (a dog)."

CONSIDER THIS!

TAKE A POSITION! Some people don't want to buy pet food. They make their own pet food. They want natural pet food. They want fresh pet food. Do you think pets should get special food? Argue your point with reasons and evidence.

SAY WHAT? Explain why people test pet food. Explain the reasons why this is a needed job.

THINK ABOUT IT! Some people think pet food is unhealthy. Pet food supporters disagree. They think being healthy doesn't matter. They think most humans don't eat healthy. They think pet food is healthier than human food. What do you think about this?

SEE A DIFFERENT SIDE! Pet owners love their pets. They spend a lot of money on their pets. They treat their pets like human kids. They buy special toys. They buy special pet food. Pet food companies make a lot of money. Some people think the companies take advantage of pet owners. Learn more about this point of view. Do you agree or disagree?

LEARN MORE: RESOURCES

PRIMARY SOURCE
Taylor-Laino, Barbara. *The Healthy Homemade Pet Food Cookbook: 75 Whole-Food Recipes and Tasty Treats for Dogs and Cats of All Ages.* Beverly, MA: Fair Winds Press, 2013.

SECONDARY SOURCES
Palika, Liz. *The Ultimate Pet Food Guide: Everything You Need to Know about Feeding Your Dog or Cat .* Cambridge, MA: Da Capo Press, 2008.
Weiskopf, Joan. *Pet Food Nation: The Smart, Easy, and Healthy Way to Feed Your Pet Now.* New York: Collins, 2007.

WEB SITES
Association for Truth in Pet Food: http://associationfortruthinpetfood.com
Association of American Feed Control Officials: www.aafco.org

GLOSSARY

gristle (GRIS-uhl) tough meat bits

gruesome (GROO-suhm) gross

ingredients (in-GREE-dee-uhnts) the things needed to make a dish

palate (PAL-it) sense of taste

premium (PREE-mee-uhm) top quality

recalled (rih-KAWLD) to have things returned

roadkill (ROHD-kil) the remains of an animal killed by a car

scraps (SKRAPS) leftovers that humans didn't finish eating

taste buds (TAYST BUDZ) small bumps on the tongue that sense flavors

umami (oo-MAH-mee) a savory flavor

INDEX

ABOUT THE AUTHOR

Dr. Virginia Loh-Hagan is an author, university professor, former classroom teacher, and curriculum designer. She'll do a lot for her pets, but she won't test their food. She lives in San Diego with her very tall husband and very naughty dogs. To learn more about her, visit www.virginialoh.com.